C000177456

THE BOOK [partly covered by label]

LOVE

LIZZIE CORNWALL

THE BOOK OF LOVE

Copyright © Summersdale Publishers Ltd, 2015

Research by Katherine Bassford

All rights reserved.

No part of this book may be reproduced by any means, nor transmitted, nor translated into a machine language, without the written permission of the publishers.

Condition of Sale
This book is sold subject to the condition that it shall not, by way of trade or otherwise, be lent, re-sold, hired out or otherwise circulated in any form of binding or cover other than that in which it is published and without a similar condition including this condition being imposed on the subsequent purchaser.

Summersdale Publishers Ltd
46 West Street
Chichester
West Sussex
PO19 1RP
UK

www.summersdale.com

Printed and bound in China

ISBN: 978-1-84953-643-1

Substantial discounts on bulk quantities of Summersdale books are available to corporations, professional associations and other organisations. For details contact Nicky Douglas by telephone: +44 (0) 1243 756902, fax: +44 (0) 1243 786300 or email: nicky@summersdale.com.

We love because it is the
only true adventure.
Nikki Giovanni

LAUGHTER BINDS PEOPLE TOGETHER. TAKE TIME TO HAVE FUN TOGETHER.

EVERY LOVE STORY IS
BEAUTIFUL, BUT OURS
IS MY FAVOURITE.

Blessed is the influence of
one true, loving human soul
on another.
George Eliot

He who walks the road
with love will never walk that
road alone again.

Charles Thomas Davis

GO OUTSIDE AND GAZE AT
THE STARS TOGETHER.

What is love? It is the morning and it is also the evening star.

Sinclair Lewis

Romance is the glamour
which turns the dust of everyday
life into a golden haze.

Elinor Glyn

REMINISCE ABOUT YOUR
FAVOURITE MEMORIES AS A COUPLE,
WHETHER IT'S YOUR FIRST DATE,
BEST HOLIDAY OR MOST
HILARIOUS DISASTER!

LOVE IS AN
ACTION VERB.

Lust is easy. Love is hard.
Like is most important.

Carl Reiner

The decision to kiss for the first time is the most crucial in any love story.

Emil Ludwig

Anyone can be passionate,
but it takes real lovers
to be silly.
Rose Franken

PRETEND YOU'RE TEENAGERS AGAIN – GO TO A FAIRGROUND AND KISS ON THE FERRIS WHEEL OR IN THE BACK ROW OF THE CINEMA.

A life without love is like a year without summer.

Swedish proverb

Everybody needs a hug.
It changes your metabolism.

Leo Buscaglia

TAKE THE TIME TO SNUGGLE WITH YOUR PARTNER BEFORE GOING TO SLEEP AT NIGHT AND BEFORE GETTING UP IN THE MORNING.

HUGS NOURISH
THE SOUL.

Let your love be like the
misty rains, coming softly,
but flooding the river.

Malagasy proverb

A kiss that speaks
volumes is seldom
a first edition.
Clare Whiting

You know you're in love
when you can't fall asleep
because reality is finally better
than your dreams.

Dr Seuss

DO SOMETHING ADVENTUROUS TOGETHER – GO SKINNY-DIPPING, ROLLER SKATING OR KAYAKING.

ALL YOU NEED IS LOVE.
THE REST IS JUST
ICING ON THE CAKE.

Life without love is like a tree
without blossoms or fruit.

Khalil Gibran

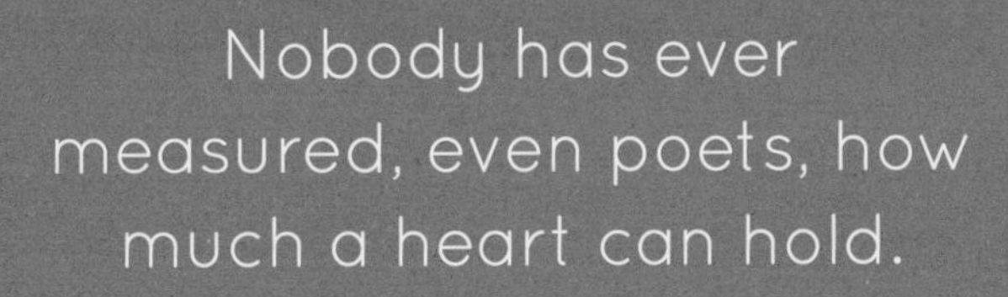
Nobody has ever
measured, even poets, how
much a heart can hold.
Zelda Fitzgerald

SEND YOUR PARTNER A POSTCARD SAYING, 'I LOVE YOU FOR A MILLION REASONS – HERE ARE THE TOP THREE...'

IT'S IMPOSSIBLE TO
LOVE SOMEONE FULLY
UNLESS YOU FULLY
LOVE YOURSELF.

There is always some madness in love. But there is also some reason in madness.

Friedrich Nietzsche

The consciousness of
loving and being loved brings
a warmth and richness to life
that nothing else can bring.

Oscar Wilde

Of all forms of caution,
caution in love is perhaps the
most fatal to true happiness.

Bertrand Russell

KEEP THE DOORS TO
YOUR HEART OPEN
AND THE WINDOWS TO
YOUR SOUL UNLOCKED.

PLAN A ROMANTIC
PICNIC JUST FOR THE
TWO OF YOU.

Affection is responsible
for nine-tenths of whatever
solid and durable happiness
there is in our lives.

C. S. Lewis

There is no surprise more magical than the surprise of being loved. It is God's finger on man's shoulder.

Charles Morgan

Love is the condition in
which the happiness of another
person is essential to your own.
Robert A. Heinlein

LEARN WHAT MAKES YOUR PARTNER FEEL LOVED, SUCH AS A CUDDLE, A LITTLE NOTE OR BREAKFAST IN BED, AND EXPRESS YOUR LOVE TO THEM IN THESE WAYS.

LOVE IS NOT WHO YOU
CAN SEE YOURSELF
WITH. IT IS WHO YOU
CAN'T SEE YOURSELF
WITHOUT.

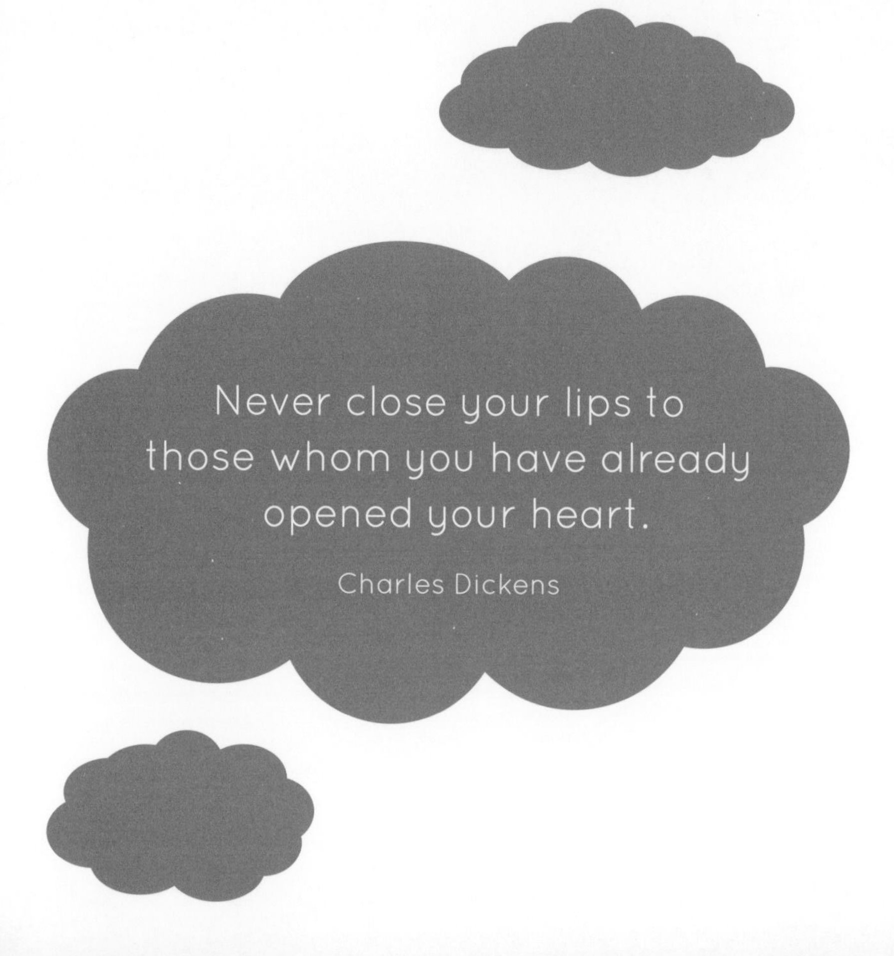
Never close your lips to
those whom you have already
opened your heart.
Charles Dickens

Love does not consist in
gazing at each other, but in
looking outward together in
the same direction.

Antoine de Saint-Exupéry

A kiss is a lovely
trick designed by nature to
stop speech when speech
becomes unnecessary.

Ingrid Bergman

EVEN WHEN YOU AND YOUR PARTNER DISAGREE, RESPECT YOUR PARTNER'S POINT OF VIEW AND ACKNOWLEDGE THE POINTS THEY MAKE. THIS IS THE BEST WAY TO REACH AN AGREEMENT.

HEALTHY RELATIONSHIPS ARE BUILT ON GIVING AND TAKING ON BOTH SIDES.

One can give without loving, but one cannot love without giving.

Amy Carmichael

There is the same difference in a person before and after he is in love as there is in an unlighted lamp and one that is burning.

Vincent van Gogh

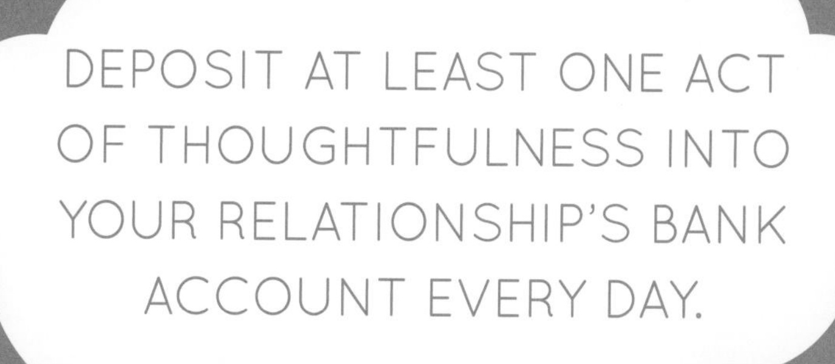
DEPOSIT AT LEAST ONE ACT
OF THOUGHTFULNESS INTO
YOUR RELATIONSHIP'S BANK
ACCOUNT EVERY DAY.

SOMETIMES YOU JUST
NEED TO HOLD EACH
OTHER'S HANDS.

Love me when I least
deserve it, because that's
when I really need it.

Swedish proverb

My heart is ever at your service.

William Shakespeare

Three things can't be hidden:
coughing, poverty and love.

Yiddish proverb

REMEMBER SOMETIMES TO
TURN OFF THE TELEVISION,
CUDDLE UP ON THE SOFA
AND TALK ALL EVENING.

THE MOST
BEAUTIFUL THING IS
SEEING THE PERSON
YOU LOVE SMILE.

Real love stories
never have endings.
Richard Bach

Sometimes the shortest distance between two points is a winding path walked arm in arm.

Robert Brault

The best thing to
hold onto in life is
each other.

Audrey Hepburn

RECREATE THE EXCITEMENT OF YOUR FIRST DATE BY GOING TO THE SAME PLACE AND EATING THE SAME FOOD – AND FALL IN LOVE ALL OVER AGAIN.

STRONG
RELATIONSHIPS
ARE BUILT ON
FOUNDATIONS OF
TRUST AND RESPECT.

Love is but the discovery of
ourselves in others, and the
delight in the recognition.

Alexander Smith

Love doesn't sit there like
a stone, it has to be made, like
bread; remade all of the time,
made new.

Ursula K. Le Guin

Being deeply loved by someone gives you strength, while loving someone deeply gives you courage.

Lao Tzu

IF YOUR PARTNER IS
HAVING A BAD DAY, TEXT
THEM A SILLY PHOTO TO
MAKE THEM SMILE.

LITTLE ACTS OF
LOVE MAKE A BIG
DIFFERENCE.

Romance is thinking
about your significant other, when
you are supposed to be thinking
about something else.

Nicholas Sparks

You come to love not by finding the perfect person, but by seeing an imperfect person perfectly.

Sam Keen

Love is a friendship
set to music.

Joseph Campbell

GO WALKING TOGETHER
HAND IN HAND, AND ENJOY
EXPERIENCING LIFE AT THE SAME
PACE AND IN CONNECTION
WITH YOUR PARTNER.

THROUGH WIND AND
RAIN LET YOUR LOVE
SHINE MORE STRONGLY
THAN EVER.

Love is composed of a single soul inhabiting two bodies.

Aristotle

Each moment of a happy lover's hour is worth an age of dull and common life.

Aphra Behn

ASK FRIENDS TO RECOMMEND THE MOST ROMANTIC RESTAURANT THEY KNOW, AND TAKE YOUR PARTNER THERE AS A SURPRISE.

NEVER FORGET YOU'RE PART OF A TEAM; YOU'RE ON THE SAME SIDE!

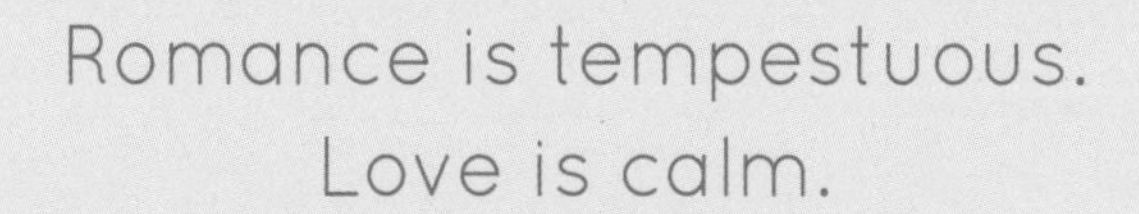

Romance is tempestuous.
Love is calm.

Mason Cooley

If grass can grow through cement, love can find you at every time in your life.

Cher

He is not a lover who
does not love forever.
Euripides

LOOK THROUGH YOUR PHOTO COLLECTION AND RELIVE THE FUN OF HOLIDAYS AND DAYS OUT TOGETHER.

DON'T LET YOUR EGO STOP YOU FROM SAYING, 'I'M SORRY,' 'I MISS YOU' OR 'I LOVE YOU'.

Love isn't something you find.
Love is something that finds you.
Loretta Young

Indeed, the ideal story is
that of two people who go
into love step by step.

Robert Louis Stevenson

A kiss makes the heart young again and wipes out the years.

Rupert Brooke

ADD SURPRISE ITEMS
TO THE WEEKLY SHOPPING
LIST, LIKE 'KISSES' OR 'A
CUDDLE FROM YOU'.

UNDERSTANDING YOUR PARTNER MEANS KNOWING THEIR FAVOURITE PIZZA TOPPING AS WELL AS THEIR HOPES AND DREAMS.

When you love someone,
all your saved-up wishes
start coming out.

Elizabeth Bowen

Love is an indescribable sensation – perhaps a conviction, a sense of certitude.

Joyce Carol Oates

Where there is love
there is no question.

Albert Einstein

MAKE YOUR PARTNER A PACKED LUNCH AND PUT A LOVING NOTE INSIDE TO SURPRISE THEM.

EVERY RELATIONSHIP
HAS UPS AND DOWNS,
IT'S HOW YOU RIDE THE
WAVES TOGETHER
THAT COUNTS.

Antoine de Saint-Exupéry

I love you – I am at rest with you – I have come home.

Dorothy L. Sayers

MAKE IT A HABIT TO INCLUDE LOVING TOUCHES IN YOUR LIFE TOGETHER EVERY DAY, SUCH AS A HUG, A KISS OR A MASSAGE.

LISTEN TO YOUR
HEART DURING TIMES
OF CONFLICT.

Life is the flower for
which love is the honey.

Victor Hugo

You never lose by loving. You always lose by holding back.
Barbara de Angelis

GIVE YOU PARTNER SOME 'LOVE VOUCHERS' AS A PLAYFUL PRESENT. THEY COULD BE FOR A MASSAGE OR A KISS, OR SOMETHING SAUCIER!

LOVE WITH ALL
YOUR HEART.

Everything is clearer
when you're in love.

John Lennon

In dreams and in love there are no impossibilities.

János Arany

The way to love anything is to realise that it may be lost.

G. K. Chesterton

IF YOUR PARTNER LOOKS WORRIED OR STRESSED LISTEN FIRST, THEN OFFER SUPPORT AND ADVICE.

TRUE LOVE IS LOVING
SOMEONE FOR WHO
THEY ARE.

Love is an act of endless
forgiveness, a tender look
which becomes a habit.

Peter Ustinov

The Eskimos had fifty-two names for snow because it was important to them: there ought to be as many for love.

Margaret Atwood

A heart that loves is always young.
Greek proverb

PUT THE BIN OUT OR DO
THE WASHING UP WHEN IT'S
YOUR PARTNER'S TURN.

HAVE FAITH. TRUST IS AN IMPORTANT INGREDIENT IN THE RECIPE OF LOVE.

The little kindnesses and courtesies are so important... In relationships, the little things are the big things.
Stephen R. Covey

One does not fall 'in' or 'out' of love. One grows in love.

Leo Buscaglia

GO ON A DATE ONCE A WEEK AND TAKE IT IN TURNS TO CHOOSE WHAT YOU DO.

IF YOU ADORE
SOMEONE, SHOW THEM.

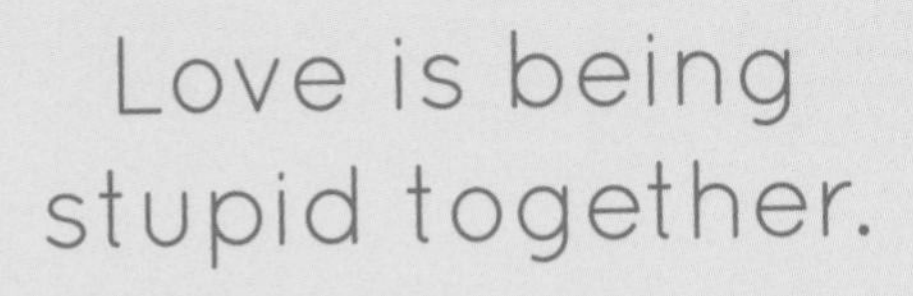
Love is being
stupid together.
Paul Valéry

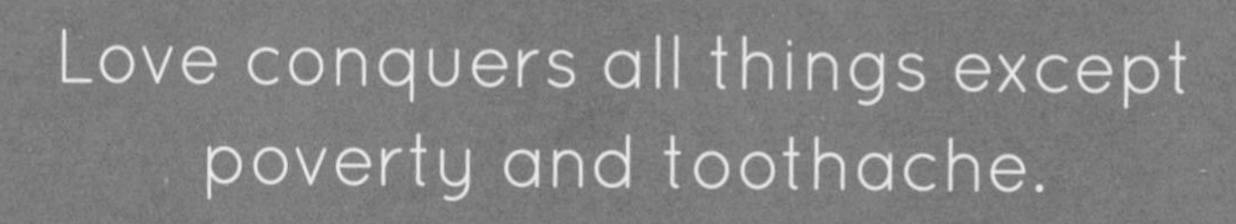

Love conquers all things except poverty and toothache.

Mae West

ASK YOURSELF EACH DAY
WHAT YOU CAN DO TO MAKE
YOUR PARTNER'S LIFE BETTER
AND SHOW THEM YOUR LOVE.

MAKE TIME TO
MAKE LOVE.

Love grows by giving. The love we give away is the only love we keep. The only way to retain love is to give it away.

Elbert Hubbard

Where there is great love,
there are always miracles.

Willa Cather

Romance is everything.

Gertrude Stein

PHONE OR TEXT JUST
TO SAY 'I LOVE YOU'.

MAKE LOVE YOUR
TOP PRIORITY.

Love is a game that two
can play and both win.

Eva Gabor

There is only one happiness in life; to love and be loved.

George Sand

INVENT YOUR OWN ROMANTIC COCKTAIL, WITH HEART-SHAPED ICE CUBES AND FRUIT CUT INTO HEARTS.

The consciousness of
loving and being loved brings a
warmth and richness to life that
nothing else can bring.

Oscar Wilde

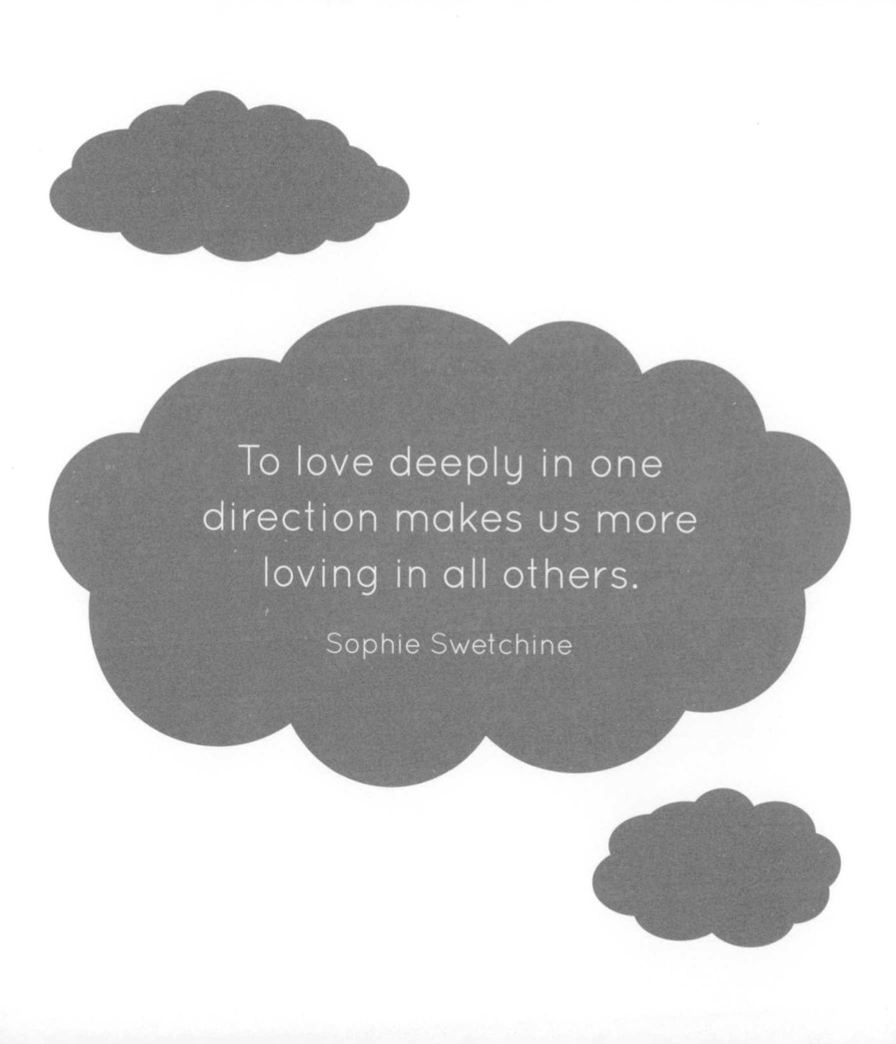
To love deeply in one direction makes us more loving in all others.
Sophie Swetchine

There is no heaven
like mutual love.

George Granville

LOVE CONQUERS ALL.

If you're interested in finding out more about our books, find us on Facebook at **Summersdale Publishers** and follow us on Twitter at **@Summersdale**.

www.summersdale.com